Shadowcatcher

So now, taking upon me the mystery of things, I could go like a spy without leaving this place, without stirring from my chair....The birds sing in chorus; the house is whitened; the sleeper stretches; gradually all is astir. Light floods the room and drives shadow beyond shadow to where they hang in folds inscrutable. What does this central shadow hold? Something? Nothing? I do not know.

Virginia Woolf, *The Waves*

Contents

Shadowcatcher

A Drawer Filled to Overflowing

It's the sails of spatulas I praise,
their sturdy masts
ready for any wind
and the Vollwrath ice cream scoop,
that clicks with perfect gears
beside the three clanking whisks
in the French style:
elegant stirrers of sauces,
of olive oil, balsamic vinegar;
beaters of eggs, next to
their coy stepsister,
the coiled whisk. I praise

the sensible wooden spoons
with their burns, stains and cracks;
their comfortable fit in any hand,
and Grandmother's ladle:
Rogers' triple plate, worn thin,
pitted by too many soups,
and the rolling pin still
smelling of butter and blueberries.

We need more in the world
that clanks, whirls and scoops.
We need the familiar,
the worn, the cracked.

We need lovely disorder;
predictable, exuberant clutter
overflowing into our hands.

Reading a Poem to Laurie

She can read my face;
eats every word
as if it were a feast,
even the smallest pause feeds her.

"It's the letters," she says,
"when I see them on a page
they dance too fast.
There's a whole world I'll never know.

But I can remember everything:
I will remember your face,
the small song of your poem.
I will remember the words,
I will remember."

Dragonfly

The piebald dragonfly hums,
moves to where
you're sanding spindles
on the lathe you've just invented
from a drill.

The dragonfly slides on the sound
the lathe makes;
embraces the vibration,
expects at any moment,
you will fly.

My Feet

know everything:
new grass, tidewash,
broken sidewalks,
leafpiles,
blackberries,
clemantines,
starfish,
stones,
chanterelles,
pomegranates,
secrets.
My feet are
the heart's navigators,
my adventure tour guides,
my sherpas.

Bad Girls

My old friend shells broad beans
from my garden,
calls them fava.
French? she asks, Italian?
It doesn't matter, I say,
if you've got garlic and basil.

We've spent the afternoon
at Otter Point
watching the comfortable fog sweep in.

She reminds me
of our halcyon days
when we dangled a mannequin's
ketchup- bloodied arm
from the trunk of the Studebaker,
drove to gas stations,
asked, " Where's the river?"

Or when we dropped ice cubes
from the 10th floor
of that Florida hotel,
then hid under the bed.
Oh, we were bad girls then.

And now, in the time between
middle and old,
we're still bad girls,
looking for the river,
waiting for the fog.

Conversation Above the Lake

"Will you sit here?" you ask me.
This is where you spend your afternoons,
watching the lake, the ospreys,
the double-crested cormorants,
in this room of silence and echo.
On the mantle, a ceramic dancer
bends in silhouette.
Your daughter, the dancer,
laughs in another room.
The voice of her sister,
who dreams of horses,
drifts in the air.
Our words move in time
to their voices,
as we waltz in and out of what matters:
what breaks the heart,
what heals it.

East of Holstein

She lived just east of Holstein,
a blue-eyed widow,
growing perennial geraniums,
iris, blue-veined squash
she covered every night
just in case of frost.

When the porcupine arrived
to eat her stairs and the corners of her house
she brought out
the old Smith & Wesson
from the wooden box in the garage
just to hold.

Tried salt licks, aged pee,
powdered orange rinds, tea bags,
ash.
Until one night
between dream and morning
she heard the crunch of wood
and as if she were asleep,
moved to the garage
and held the cold metal.

Later, she said
the porcupine was gone;
meaning, buried deep
under the iris;
never said she shot it.
Never said,
when the iris bloomed
the next spring,
spiked with white and black.
She never said.

Poem in Reply to an E-mail

You send greetings: an e-mail
on my birthday; assure me
this will be a year to remember.

I want to tell you, it's the days
I want to remember:
the late November walk with my friend,
past two old guys sawing alder on the beach,
past clam shells wrapped in bear scat,
past the maple thick with moss,
past owl scat filled with the fine bones of mice;
whole small skeletons.

I want to tell you,
it's the ordered geese on the lawn,
the hesitant moon,
the small skeletons
I want to remember.

Luminous Storms

I've lived in the house on the Strait for thirty years.
Watched the west winds bend in the windows
each winter; have eaten the luminous storms, the terrible rain.
The wind drove the husbands I have forgotten
from the house; they couldn't hear
the wind's language.
Or know what I heard: the scavenging gulls,
their mad circling; the wren's small songs
hidden in the November wood. I'm in flight
at the end of love; at its beginning.

Bear, Hurricane, Rain

Just walk until you're hungry.
Fried squid and a jug of cheap wine in a two table café,
under a washline of bleached sheets—
these can help you stop dying for a while.
                    Douglas Burnet Smith, "A Postage Stamp"

This is not a poem about a bear,
who ambled past
the backyard honeysuckle,
toward the room filled with the smell
of Gravenstein apples.
He pushed open the door,
began to eat.
We heard him,
watched for a while, said,
just walk until you're hungry.

This is not a poem about a hurricane,
that took the elms and poplars
of the Halifax Public Gardens
and turned them into dead giants
behind a locked, wrought iron cage.
Later, the candlelight people
came out of their houses, weeping,
moved into the sun,
and somehow found
fried squid and a jug of cheap wine in a two table café.

This is not a poem about rain,
that fell with a kind of music
no one had heard before:
all timpani and cello,
beating its own rhythm on the earth,
until the earth became
a song of water,
and we waited, waited,
to sit again
under a washline of bleached sheets.

This is a poem about a bear, a hurricane, and rain
and all that makes our hearts beat,
our hearts break.
This is a poem about
all that is wild,
full of wind and water, about
apples, honeysuckle,
elms, poplars, cellos, drums:
these can help you stop dying for a while.

Cafe Vienna, Halifax

The woman at the Café Vienna
tells me she's going to "give a woolen"
to her no-good husband Bud,
who's out drinking beer, or worse,
would you believe it?

The scent of Tide washes up
from the Blue Nose Laundromat below.
She tells me her name is Crystal;
she's from Folly Lake.
The tattoo on her arm reads,
"Bud, I love you, you son of a bitch."

She wants to tell me her story.
But I'm not ready for her ship of tears.
I'm thinking of the Viennese waltzes
I'll never dance to
and the tattoos I never had
the courage to wear.

I'm thinking of the maple
I planted from a winged seed
one spring,
so full now of green buds,
rain.

Carmen Doesn't Know Bizet

or much about gypsies,
orange sellers, toreadors.
She's not the kind of gal
who would discard men
like flowers.

She's Carmen of the 5 Cents to a Dollar Store,
in downtown Antigonish.
She knows a lot about
the batteries, shaver heads
and blank CD's
that line the shelves behind her.

She looks at the page of panties
from Fashion Magazine
I ask her to copy.

She says she'd wear Escada's Flora Delight,
if she had 95 bucks to buy them,
or Joe Boxer's Pina Coladas
decorated with a golden pineapple,
or Calvin Klein's Garden Party.
If she had $230, she'd go for
Lis Charmel's Spring Bouquet,
all lace and sweet ribbons.

For now, she says
she'll buy a package of Hanes Her Way,
for sure, every year.
White cotton;
something she can trust,
something she'd be proud to be seen in,
if she got knocked over by a bus
of if the wind came up and whipped
her skirt around.

But, she says,
she might save up
for La Senza's Lily Pad,
just for the name,
for all the lovely flowers.

Water Putty

I'm waiting in line at Home Hardware
to buy a can of Durham's Water Putty.
The guy in front of me offers his two cents:
says it fixed his door knobs just like that.
Then the lady behind me says she wants a can
for her creaky chairs.
Someone behind her says he'll take some too,
and asks if he knows me from somewhere.
Hey, I'm just here for some rock hard water putty,
made in Des Moines, Iowa.
By now I'm ready to buy some stock.
I hold the can for everyone to see;
meets a thousand repair needs—
indispensable I tell them:
something that sticks, stays put
and will not shrink, in this loose,
crumbling, dispensable world.

It's the Heat

It's 37 degrees in Kamloops
and there's nothing like a breeze;
the air feels like a winter coat
and I'm thinking about getting
a dolche latte gelato
when 4 cop cars pull up
and 8 cops jump out,
manhandle a guy,
handcuff him.
2 minutes later they let him go.
It's the heat, I say.
Then a junkie on rollerblades
sweeps in for a smoothie,
and I take off for VV Boutique.
The guy next to me
in sandals and a skirt
wants my opinion
of the black size 14 cocktail dress
with a flared hem,
well, I say, does it fit?
Sure, he says,
sometimes I can wear a 12.
It's the heat, I say.
Then the kid who
plays a tune on a toy
featured above a rack of pants
tells me he wants to be in a rock band,
needs some green pants
and finds them,
the colour of parrot's wings.

It's the heat, I say.
Up and down Victoria Street
are bald guys
and their shining motorcycles.
The air rises from them
as if they were a mirage.
It's the heat, I say,
it's the heat.

Phone Booth

I was downtown and
had to use a payphone.
There was a note taped
to the glass which read:
"My television's broken,
I'm lonely.
I read palms, tell balmy fortunes,
call me up."

I did. A guy answered.
He said, "For 10 bucks I'll read your palm."
I asked, "Will you read both for 15?"

We met at Starbucks.
He looked poetic, morally angelic.
He was 39, unemployed,
delicious.
He wore interesting glasses
left over from a more
prosperous life.

He read my right palm:
"You will have money in the bank,
learn to tap dance,
grow a big garden.
This year, you'll get squash."

Then he read my left palm:
"You will not travel
around the world by Concorde.
You will own a Pashmina shawl
the colour of faded lilac.
A guy with interesting glasses
will ask you for a date."

Which he did.

I bought him a big plasma TV.
We grew squash for years.

Dreaming of Stephen Dunn at a Poetry Retreat

I'm in the middle of a dream
when you open the door
and you tell me it's time to get up.
This morning of fog,
I move down the stairs.

I'm still thinking of the cop
outside the poetry café, whom I've
just approached in the dream,
and have questions he doesn't want to hear,
like, why are you here?
This is a poetry reading, I tell him,
where nothing more dangerous
than a mixed metaphor is likely
to disrupt the room.
I notice he has a silver badge
that says " stop it",
which is lit up like Christmas,
with little red flashing lights,
as if he were his own police car.
And I suddenly see that he looks
a lot like Stephen Dunn and he tells
me that he's just been to the Laundromat
down the block, checking out what
the gals are putting into the dryer's
delicate cycle.
Then I see he is Stephen Dunn,
and I tell him I was just going
to send him a letter,
enclose my poems about Fred Astaire,
whom we both think is the cat's ass.
Then the door opens,
you say, "awake, awake, the dawn is here,
the world is full of atmosphere".
I believe you.

Dinner With Fred

I'd like to have dinner with Fred Astaire,
that lovely boulevardier,
at the Paris Ritz.
He'd move his elegant hands
when he ordered the wine,
enthrall the waiters.

Oh Fred, I'd say,(imagining
I was Cyd Charisse,
who had beautiful legs)
will you show me how
to dance on the ceiling,
because, well, it's been
a dream of mine for forty years?

He'd move to the walls,
and up he'd go to the chandelier;
the whole place
would rattle,
plaster falling into the caviar.
He'd stretch out his arms,
and I'd be there with Fred,
upside down,
seeing the world
as it really is.

Monandry

I found the word, "monandry",
and thought of the good, monandrous life
I've led; one husband
at a time.
And thought how the word could break apart
in a moment: "mon"(Monday) "and" , "dry".

Monday and dry, no rain,
the clear moon and oh the stars,
did you see Orion, I asked him,
my Monday husband,
thinking of the Argentinean
I met one night in New York,
who invited me for champagne and tango.
Well, I told myself, he didn't count.
I was still monandrous, like a flower
with one perfect stamen. A stargazer,
a lily.

Calling Harry

When Harry got sick,
he took advantage of technology
or technology took advantage of him,
according to Rose.

He got a silver cell phone,
called every business under "B"
in the yellow pages:
bakeries, barbers, balloons,
bankruptcy guys,
bank machine salesmen,
beauty parlours,
bike shops, bookstores,
purveyors of brass fasteners.

He sat all day in his navy blue
Lazy boy, wearing a red golf cap
that never left his head in daylight;
started each conversation with,
"So how's business?"
Then he placed an order if he could.

Rose would open the door
to a hundred coloured balloons
shaped like the moon,
a dozen marzipan cakes inscribed with
"I love you, Baby"
a tandem bike,
and a gross of brass fasteners.

When Rose buried Harry,
she lifted the coffin's lid,
placed the cell phone by his ear.

She called him every day;
even when the phone lost its charge,
said that she had wanted to say more,
but never had the words,
and swore if she got the chance
or the courage,
she'd tell him she loved it all:
the cakes, balloons, brass fasteners;
how she loved him.
Harry.

A Cure for Melancholy

Wear a necklace of broken bells.
Listen to the nightbirds
and their long silence.
Speak to the kitchen ghosts.
Wash fear from the steps
with lemons and violets.
Find the feather of a white crow,
hide it.
Watch the sky.

Spiders

It is September,
the month of conflagrations,
spiders.
I watch a tortoise shell spider
spin his web
between the manure pile and the Scotch broom.
He's upside down,
sideways in the wind;
sometimes a dancer in the sun,
sometimes a tightrope walker.

I'm thinking of Phillipe Petit,
who, with three hundred feet of one inch wire
and a bow and arrow,
joined the space between the Twin Towers,
and stepped a quarter mile into the sky.
He balanced on the border
of what he could imagine.
Sometimes, he went down on one knee;
sometimes, he lay down on the wire.

When he saw a bird with clear red eyes,
so close he could hear its wingbeat,
he knew that he had woven his dream,
balanced on it, had made a fine, silver web.

Green Bean Princess

I wanted to be a magic carpet rider;
take off over the rooftops
like some highflying Chagall sweetheart,
wearing rubies and a red dress,

take off over the rooftops.
Instead, I am the green bean princess,
wearing rubies and a red dress,
the rhubarb queen.

Instead, I am the green bean princess,
I'm rooted as a beet in my old garden,
the rhubarb queen;
poems fly like Monarchs.

I'm rooted as a beet in my old garden.
In the apple trees,
poems fly like Monarchs.
Sometimes I wear diamonds

in the apple trees
like some highflying Chagall sweetheart.
Sometimes I wear diamonds.
I wanted to be a magic carpet rider.

Harbour's Edge

I walk to the harbour's edge,
watch two swimmers half way out.
I hold their clothes.
I wait.

Watch two swimmers half way out.
There is always time for waiting.
I wait.
It's safe to wait at the edge.

There is always time for waiting
behind fear's broken fence.
It's safe to wait at the edge.
But if the heat sings

behind fear's broken fence
in the middle of the day,
but if the heat sings,
hear yes; hear water. Swim.

In the middle of the day
I hold their clothes,
hear yes; hear water. Swim.
I walk to the harbour's edge.

Tapestries

She tells me she doesn't want to bare her soul.
But sings of her rainbow chard,
raspberries, beets,
her delicata squash.

But sings of her rainbow chard,
and oh, the dark green beauties,
her delicata squash
she tells me their secrets.

And oh, the dark green beauties,
the looms that fill her house,
she tells me their secrets,
these tapestries;

the looms that fill her house
and what she imagines:
these tapestries
in the garden between sleep and dream.

And what she imagines:
raspberries, beets,
in the garden between sleep and dream.
She tells me she doesn't want to bare her soul.

Roses

On the lake's stony beach
are three fleshy gals,
sitting in florescent exuberance
as they watch me swim by.
Ahead, there's a heron,
matching the shadows;
a hawk
flying wide
under the waiting moon.

It's not summer yet:
but in the garden,
the roses, big as melons,
bend the branches.
I swim past the women
in magenta, scarlet, electric lemon,
sitting there; three roses,
passing the fragrant day,
waiting for the moon.

Wrong to the Eye

*A coleus, wrong to my eye because its leaves
were red, was rooting on the sill.*
Jane Kenyon

The cat's decapitated a bird.
The broken wing hides the blood
with brilliant feathers.

The sun near solstice
turns the sky to blood and gold.
My eyes burn, waiting for alchemy.

Along the path by the shore,
rosehips and snowberries in the sun;
everywhere there are signs I can't read.

The goose with the broken leg stumbles on the grass.
I want to help, offer bread.
I stand by the last red leaves of autumn, watch.

Starfish

These are the five pointed
spaceships of the tide,
waiting for the clams
they will pull apart
to make new galaxies
on the waves
that wash and wash;
such exquisite, symmetrical death.

She Carried Her Pain in Her Prada Bag

black leather, with golden stars on the strap,
the clasp, a silver moon.
In each compartment
were polite letters
written on Crane's Distaff Linen, addressed
to her children,
her friends,
her hairdresser;
enough pills
to die quietly
in a hotel room somewhere;
a photograph of her
taken last July
wearing her mauve Versace dress.
She carried all the words
she could never say
in her Prada bag;
her silence wrapped
in red silk,
as if it were a gift.

Rings: Youth Court, St. Albert, Alberta

I see the scars that circle her wrist,
and the fourteen rings she wears.
Amanda says she's fifteen:
she never asked about the cars
Brandon stole;
never asked about the silver Trans Am
he drove for a day,
or the red Mustang, the next.
She's already learned
love's sad tricks:
to bury, be silent,
and pretend.
Her eyes never
leave the door.
She says she's been to this court
before,
last year,
to put her brother in jail
for what he did,
what he did.
And she looks again
toward the guarded door,
ringed in scars.

The Stoning of Shemsiye Allack

I think the room is blue,
or the ceiling is blue,
and I don't know if you can see it,
through the tubes
and the blur of your mind.

The day they brought you to the wall,
pregnant from the rape,
the sky was blue,
the Turkish air
smelled of oil and poppies.

They said, the ones who held the stones,
that you had shamed them.

The stones fell on you
like a terrible rain
and broke you,
and your mind ran out in streams
and your memory became a dry lake of blood.

You didn't die.
You lie alone,
in this blue room.
Shemsiye Allack.

Hamburg, July 28, 1943

I can see, but cannot read
a child's small death.
Why do they hold us,
why do they tear at the heart?
                    Patrick Lane, *Fragments*

First the windows were blown from their frames,
then the doors.
The bombs took whole attic floors.
The fires became a sea of heat:
a searing storm.
It was 1:20 a.m.
Flames reached a mile into the sky.
Roofs and gables flew in the air.
Whole trees were torn from the ground.
I can see but cannot read

so much pain.
I look at the photograph:
two women in black push a wooden cart
piled with mattresses, eiderdowns,
suitcases with shining brass locks.
A man, too old for this task,
a husband, pulls the cart;
he wears heavy shoes.
They are already blind to
a child's small death.

If they see a woman carrying
the charred corpse of her child,
they do not remember.
They see what is broken;
what remains:
the rise of an arch, a cornice, a balustrade.
They see past the burning,
the stones, the heaps of bone,
rubble, ash.
Why do they hold us?

I want to name them:
Anna, for my grandmother,
Tanta, for my great aunt,
Victor, for my grandfather.
Will they every dance again
or dream without fire?
Will they ever sit at a wooden table,
take tea and almond cake
in the afternoon?
Why do they tear at the heart ?

Swimming With the Seals

After the surgery, after the radiation,
after the expected pain that
arrived with every step,
(like the mermaid who gave up
her voice for legs
to dance with the prince)
she gave up her fear for fins.

She walked into the sea,
seamed in neoprene,
to swim with the seals.

First, at night,
alone with the moon,
she learned to sing underwater.

Later, in daylight,
seals swam with her,
led her to beds of sea urchins, starfish.
She swam through schools
of shining fish,
sang to them;
a mermaid,
swimming toward the shore.

Before

This is how it happens:
one day you've gone to trade
The Fisherman's Encyclopedia
that you'll never read
for a copy of *The History of Roses*
and someone says,
"Have you heard about Michael?"
You know that the next sentence
will be the terrible one,
beginning with sarcoma,
ending with terminal.

It's January, all salt and sorrow.
You know then you'll visit
with cold hands and wrong words,
take a warm rice pudding,
sit close.
Watch him breathe out fear
when he tells you about
the small bed in the middle of the room
on loan from the Red Cross.
And the Dilaudid
that would cost $1000 a month
without the new provincial program.
"Palliative," he'll say,
"yes, palliative"
and his voice will disappear
somewhere into the afternoon.
And you'll get up to leave,
promise to return,
"before," you'll say,
"before," and you'll touch his burning hand.

Lunch

Michael moves from chair to table
for his lunch:
chicken noodle soup from a can;
it takes all the effort he has to move three feet.
He talks about his Christian sister
who's sending him
epistles in the mail;
she knows if he embraces Jesus
he won't die.
It's too late, he says.
The Dilaudid's already lost its punch.

Spring is pretending to arrive:
sending out the early bees,
the fragrant clematis,
cherry blossoms.
He pretends to see it,
as his words thin toward sleep.

Waiting for the Whales

Michael tells me he's had
three pain free days.
He can now walk to the deck,
sit in the Adirondack chair
thick with pillows.
He's already seen a passing otter,
three black rabbits the colour of the world,
a halcyon, nesting on the sea.
He's waiting for the whales
to swim by;
to offer him esteem, magic, life.
He thinks the whales will sing to him
with words that he can understand.
And I have songs for them,
he says, whole sonatas
filled with elderberries,
amaryllis, frogs.
Whole sonatas.

Michael Rowing

Your bones break
between dreams of contrails
and the shadow of the new moon.
You imagine you are rowing
an old white boat, watching geese stand,
balance on one leg,
guard the lake.

First, it's your femur,
that long bone
without poetry.
After a month, you come home,
pinned and plated,
filled with methadone,
to guard against the pain
that washes in every afternoon.

You want more than
your small bed allows.
You don't say sarcoma.
You say you want to drive
to the Pacific,
see the surf break.
Eat ice cream.

You say, "This is my boat.
This is where I row."

Christmas

At night, the neighborhood's
decorated for Christmas:
the rooftops are clean angles
of blue light;
the trees take on a shining
symmetrical life,
next to golden reindeer and
red angels.

Down the road,
at the Baptist church
is a Bethlehem Walk,
with a borrowed donkey,
carols.

Your Christmas decorations
are 25 syringes of hydromorphone
in cut crystal
on the kitchen counter.
Outside , a sign on the door
says "No Visitors".

You're in the jumbled tunnel
between life and death;
only your terrible breathing
singing through the dark.

Cremating Dave

When your time is up,
it's up,
my mother says;
she knows how many ghosts
walk with her.

She would have approved of Dave's death.
His heart gave out at 52;
he died before he reached the floor.
A surprising death for a man
who loved the grace of numbers
and the seasons of his life.

Before they cremated Dave,
they dressed him
in his best Hawaiian shirt,
blooming with plumeria and birds of paradise;
placed *The Lonely Planet Guide to the Cayman Islands*
in his hands;
put two Cuban cigars
and a cheque for a million bucks in his pocket.

His time was up,
my mother would say,
a good, clean death.
All that's left:
memory, ash.

Radio Man

for David Grierson

For years, I checked my watch
by your voice;
always knew when it was 10 a.m.
Pacific Standard Time.
Later, you were the CBC morning voice
of cellos and apples:
the man with perfect questions,
laughter; more grace
than I could hold at 7 a.m.
Once you let me read this line
on air:
"she bared her plum blossom bottom"
which I thought was shocking,
and you didn't.

Today, thinking of you,
I watch 12 crows
in the November maple.
They are still as grief,
waiting in the rain.

I Want to Think

they met at a dinner dance
for Jewish young people
at the LaSalle Hotel
in South Bend, Indiana in 1938,
where orange sherbert
was served between courses.

My father wore a new serge suit.
My mother wore a buttoned silk blouse,
a rose on her wrist.
She could speak some Hungarian then,
knew how to make chopped liver,
chicken soup.
Drove a Studebaker. Was smart.
Never beautiful.

They danced, or tried to.
She listened to him talk:
economics, history.
Heard his opinions,
smiled. She was ready
to be a wife.

They were briefly perfect.

They would be terrible parents.
It wouldn't be their fault.
My father would always be
somewhere else.
My mother would be distracted,
or playing golf.

I would be saved by Annie Mae Murray,
my nanny,
who couldn't read,
but taught me the poetry
of family secrets,
washed my mouth out with soap,
always told the truth.

I want to think of my parents
still dancing at the LaSalle Hotel,
between courses,
perfect.

The Kitchen

There's not much in her kitchen now:
the green tin canisters
of flour, salt, sugar
are filled with old letters,
bits of twine,
chocolate she's hidden
from herself.

In the oven:
pans she never uses,
and a dead plant meant for the trash.
She likes cooked chicken
and one small plastic container
of macaroni and cheese,
from the supermarket,
she'll call dinner,
if she remembers.

If she remembers
the days when she could make
chicken soup, chopped liver,
pecan puffs and the kitchen steamed
with 100 recipes that got lost somewhere,
got lost.

The River

says wash, whisper. The ducks
wait at the crumbling bank.
I watch them drive and shake.
My mother can't see them,
from where she sits on her back porch.
I've brought her wildflowers
from the river's edge:
asters, goldenrod, a wild rose.
She's worried I've stolen them.
Her mind fills up with whispers,
questions wash again.
She asks,
as if for the first time,
did you steal them,
did you steal?

Clare's Heart

is made of trout fishing
on Drag Lake with the backwood boys;
is made of the sound of his skates
on the pond's blue ice;
and the three centuries
he's seen pass:
the world that has changed
and broken and changed again;

is made of the red dreams
of horses; the dark gardens of war;
his Helen's gardens of heliotrope,
hyacinth, mimosa;
all the silver ghosts that listen for their names;
his golden letters from the Queen;

is made of hockey nights on the CBC
with a couple of Molson lites.
This battered pallete.
Clare's heart.

For the Child I Never Had

If I could have made you,
you would have been
a girl with charcoal eyes
and smoky wings;
and if you had dreams,
it would be dreams of rooftops,
chimneys.
You would be my raven girl,
calling from the Sitka spruce.

I would have called you
from the branches,
I would have called you
from the green nights;
if I could have made you,
you would sing.

Star

This was the autumn he learned
to read the stars:
found Orion and Sirius;
learned the beautiful names:
Cappella, Lacerta, Aquila.
This was the year of Halley's comet.

He waited for shooting stars,
made of ice and dust.
This was 1986,
the year of his daughter's birth.
He named her Hayley,
for the comet he imagined.

Later, he showed her Pegasus,
the sky's winged horse;
knowing that one day
she would stream across
life's brilliant sky
riding horses she would name
Starburst, Stardust,
Starlight Express.

Bloom

If you were here now,
I'd show you the garden:
the rhubarb, its first leaves
waiting in small green fists.

And the daphne,
you know its perfume.

Can you remember
how the soil felt
in your hands
and how you once took
my small hands;
held them in the earth,
waiting for me to bloom?

Patrick Lane at Glenairley

6 a.m. The house is still enough
for you to hear dreams move
in small breaths down the stairs.

You stir the coffee you've just made,
wait for a sweep of sandpipers
to skim the shore.

You watch a gull in flight
begin its cerulean day
dropping a clam
onto the rocks.
You drop the spoon you hold,
the dreams you hold,
and write this line:
"He picked up the spoon from among all the small things".

Not This Garden

Not the perfect beds
of love lies bleeding,
or the bellflowers,
or the purple foxglove.
Not a sound from the bells of Ireland
or the bee balm. Or the heliotrope.
There is no wind here,
to bring the fragrant mirabilis, sweet rocket,
anise hyssop.
No.

I want disorder: death, wind, storm.
I want this February garden by the sea:
the fine decay of maple leaves,
their opaque tracery among
the rosehips, a heartbeat in winter,
and hemlock
that catches bleached seaweed
in its branches;
moss hanging
on the north side of everything.

I want the sea's garden on the shore:
crab legs like magnolia petals,
mussel shells that hold the sky;
a broken plate ringed with cornflowers,
a branch, rich with lichen.

From this garden,
the cormorant opens and closes
its wings like a fan.
I watch the heron skim the shore
and the raucous geese land.
I watch for wind, for spring;
take slow, salty breaths.

Inca Cat

The cat's in his Inca days;
presents us with
a beheaded rat,
heart missing.

We applaud this
backstep sacrifice.
He doesn't notice;
leaps to the gate
to watch the gulls
who cry in raucous profusion
on the Strait.
The cat hears this cacophony;
beats his tail in time.

The tide is rich with deadheads,
kelp beds, herring.
Winter waits in the west.
Everywhere is rain.
The cat waits golden,
full of heart.

Weathervanes

I want weathervanes:
cast iron whales
to spin in the wind.
And an angel in stone
to announce each day.

I want my bones to show
so anyone could name them:
heartbone, painbone,
soulbone, deathbone.

I want to say words
like Vilcabamba,
Madagascar,
Chiang Mai,
that fill my mouth
with exotic geography.

I want to fill up my dreams
with windchimes,
birdseed,
pinto beans,
bones.

Delicata

I am a woman who shops
at the Red Barn
for bargin broccoli, kiwi, limes.
I stop by a blue tarp,
lift it to see a symphony
of delicata squash.
I fill my basket.
My cell phone rings,
plays a tinny, insistent Ode to Joy.
I am a woman singing,
of the delicata,
green and golden in the January rain:
a madrigal, a medley,
an aria,
a poem.

How He Loved the Light

for Patrick Heron

It's enough to know
how he loved the light
and the stone house
on the rocky sweep to the sea.

It's enough to know
that the doorways
framed his art
and his garden of azaleas, camellias,
violet cobalt rhodendrons.

It's enough to know
he planted the gardens of his horizons
in lime, blue, scarlet,
emerald, lemon,
deep cadmium, ceruleum,
vermilion, aquamarine.

It's enough to know
that he loved his beautiful fictions,
his stony, glowing world.

The Path

Your life is only partially yours:
it belongs to your Yugoslavian grandfather
who came to Canada with twenty-five cents
in his pocket,
got on the wrong train,
arrived in Kapuskasing,
stood outside the mill
until he got a job.
Worked hard. Saved.
Brought over his wife
and the son he'd never seen
(who would be your father).
Took in borders.
And your father stayed,
became an engineer,
eloped with the beautiful Norwegian,
your mother.

You remember
Saturday family lunches,
where the women cooked
and the tables were filled
with stuffed peppers,
steamed lamb with cabbage,
potato dumplings,
drum cake.
Your grandmother would say
to even the fattest relative,
"eat, skeleton, eat".

Your life is only partially yours.
Your life is your grandfather's,
your grandmother's,
and the grief of their memories.
Your life is your father's;
his memories of mountains,
and your mother's;
her memories of fjords.
Your life is Yugoslavia,
your life is Norway.
Your life is the path of shadows
you walk between them.

Acknowledgements:

Some of these poems have appeared in the following magazines: *Dalhousie Review, Quills, Storm, Event, Conde Nast Traveller*, UK . Other poems have appeared in the chapbooks published by Leaf Press: *Masks, Letters We Never Sent* and *Briefly Perfect.* They have also appeared in the *Edmonton Stroll of Poets Anthology.*

These poem owe much to the encouragement and help of my companion, Rod Punnett, and to the inspired guidance of Patrick Lane, at whose poetry retreats many of these poems were written.

I'd like to thank WestJet Airlines, who have allowed me to become their poet of the skies in celebration of literacy. As well, I'd like to thank Daimler-Chrylser for providing me with a PT Cruiser into my first forays into the lovely world of Random Acts of Poetry in the Maritimes and in Ontario. As well, I thank the Fairmont Hotels, who allow me luxurious accomodations when I travel for poetry, and Prairie Naturals Vitamins who have provided me their products that keep me healthy. Abebooks deserves special thanks for supporting the National Random Acts of Poetry Week, along with The Victoria READ Society for their enthusiasm for this project.

Finally, I want to thank the following: my kind-hearted publisher, Richard Olafson; Jim Bertolino, for allowing me to steal his line "she bared her plum blossom bottom" in "Radioman"; my superb editor, Susan Stenson, whose suggestions I nearly always followed; all my poetry friends at Mocambopo for their enthusiastic support, their marvellous writing and CBC Radio's David Grierson, whose voice, filled with cellos and apples, is still remembered.